What's in this book

学习内容 Contents   2

读一读 Read   4

听听说说 Listen and say   12

写一写 Write   16

多元学习 Connections   18

温习 Checkpoint   20

分享 Sharing   22

This book belongs to

_____

我们去购物 Going shopping

学习内容 Contents

沟通 Communication

说说购物经历
Talk about shopping experiences

说说衣物
Talk about clothes

生词 New words

★	衣服	clothes
★	裤子	trousers
★	跑步	to run
★	买	to buy
★	忙	busy
★	累	tired
★	为什么	why
	爱	to like
	卖	to sell
	运动服	sportswear
	电影	film

背景介绍：
浩浩一家在家里观看体育比赛节目。

2

句式 Sentence patterns

为什么?
Why?

文化 Cultures

环球购物
Shopping around the world

跨学科学习 Project

设计手机购物应用程序的主页
Design the main page for a mobile
phone shopping application

参考答案:
1 They are watching a basketball match.
2 It is football/badminton.
3 We go shopping/go to the park.

Get ready

1 What TV programme is Hao Hao's family watching?

2 What is your favourite sport?

3 How do you and your family spend the weekends?

故事大意：
周末，爸爸妈妈带浩浩玲玲到商场买夏季运动服，并看了场电影。

pǎo bù
跑步

参考问题和答案：

1 What sports do Ling Ling and Hao Hao like? (Ling Lir likes running and Hao Hao likes playing basketball.)

yī fu
衣服

2 Do you think they need new sports clothes for summer? Why? (Yes. Because Ling Ling's jogging suit is too thick and Hao Hao's basketball jersey is too small.)

姐姐爱跑步，我爱打篮球。夏天来了，我们没有新衣服。

Sports Zone

máng
忙
"忙"用来形容
事情很多。

mǎi
买

参考问题和答案：

1　What do you think Hao Hao's family is doing in the Sports Zone?
　　(They want to buy sports clothes for the summer.)
2　What is the black woman doing? (She is buying some clothes.)
3　The man in the cap is counting some shoe boxes. Do you think
　　he is busy? (Yes, he is.)

星期六，爸爸妈妈都不忙，我们一起去买运动服。

Cashier

"卖"和"买"是一对反义词。

mài
卖

kù zi
裤子

"裤子"是笼统的叫法。玲
玲拿着的是短裤（shorts）。
长裤是trousers。

参考问题和答案：

1 Is the woman with a ponytail buying or selling
   things? (She is selling something to the customer.)
2 What is Ling Ling holding? (She is holding
   a pair of shorts.)
3 Is Ling Ling selling the shorts? (No, she is not.)

"这条裤子真可爱！"姐姐说。
"我们问问怎么卖。"妈妈说。

参考问题和答案：

1　What is Hao Hao doing? (He is holding two basketball jerseys and asking the others for their opinions.)
2　Which one do you think Hao Hao will buy? (He will buy the blue/red one.)

"这两件球衣怎么样？红色好看还是蓝色好看？"我问大家。

参考问题和答案：

1 Where is Hao Hao's family? (They are walking past the ticket office of a cinema.)
2 How does Ling Ling look? (She looks tired.)
3 What are Hao Hao and Dad looking at? (They are looking at the poster of a film.)

"买衣服比做运动累。为什么？"姐姐问。

我们用"为什么"来询问原因。"为什么"可以如上方句子单独使用，也可以放在问句里边。如：为什么买衣服比做运动累？

"因为你走了很多路。休息一下，我们去看电影吧。"爸爸说。

Let's think

1 Recall the story and circle the correct letters.

1　玲玲喜欢做什么？

a　　　　　ⓑ　　　　　c

2　星期六，浩浩、玲玲和爸爸妈妈去了哪里？

a　　　　　b　　　　　ⓒ

2 What items do you and your parents usually buy together? Tick and say.

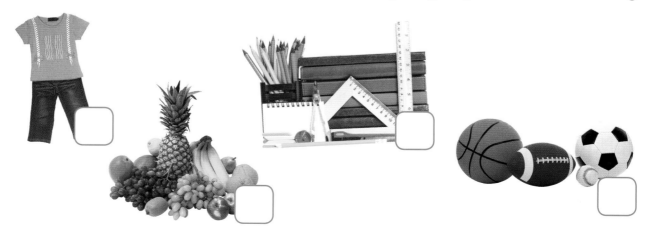

New words

1 Learn the new words.

There are two suns. Why?

2 Look at your teacher. Which word is he/she acting out? Have a guess and say it in Chinese.

延伸活动：
学生看图说话。如：浩浩和爸爸买衣服。浩浩买运动服，爸爸买裤子。他卖衣服。狗妈妈很忙。狗姐姐很累。狗弟弟说："我爱跑步。"狗爸爸说："有两个太阳。为什么？"

衣服

裤子

买

卖

运动服

电影

为什么？

忙

累

我爱跑步。

听听说说 Listen and say

第一题录音稿：

1 我们爱跑步。星期日早上，爸爸妈妈
浩浩和我都不忙。大家去跑步。

2 爸爸妈妈的运动服是蓝色的，很好看
浩浩的黄色衣服也好看。

3 我和布朗尼一起跑，真累！

03 **1** Listen and circle the correct pictures.

04 **2** Look at the pictures. Listen to the story a

1 星期日，大家一起做什么？

2 爸爸妈妈的运动服是什么颜色的？

 真累！

 为什么？

3 谁很累？

第3小题学生需要弄清楚"我"是谁。录音中出现了爸爸、妈妈和浩浩，所以"我"是玲玲。

 我没有运动服。

 为什么？

 因为我太忙了，没去买。

告诉学生运动时最好穿运动服装
因为其设计和物料更符合各种运
的特点和要求，所以比普通服装
适合运动时穿着。

第二题参考问题和答案：

1 Why is Ivan not wearing any sports clothes?
(Because he is busy running and playing basketball.)

2 Do you wear sports clothes when doing sports?
(Yes, I do./No, I do not.)

 因为我跑步了。

 你的运动服呢？

 你忙什么？

 跑步、打篮球……我爱打
篮球！

第三题参考表达：

1 因为他很忙。

2 它很高兴。为什么？
因为它爱跑步。

3 他们也很高兴。为什么？
因为他们有新衣服。

3 Look at the pictures and discuss with your friend.

1

💬 他为什么不去玩？

💬 因为他……

2

💬 它很高兴。……

💬 因为它爱……

3

💬 他们也很高兴。……

💬 ……

Task

What do you do on weekends? Draw a picture or paste a photo below and talk to your friend.

参考表达见下。

我喜欢星期六。

我喜欢……

你喜欢星期六还是星期日？

为什么？

因为……

因为我爱打球。星期六爸爸不忙，我们一起打球。

Game

鼓励学生用中文回答问题，但如果某些表达没学过，也可用英文表述。
参考答案：
我喜欢跑步，因为跑步比买衣服好玩。/我喜欢买衣服，因为跑步很累。

Find a way out of the maze and answer the cat's questions.

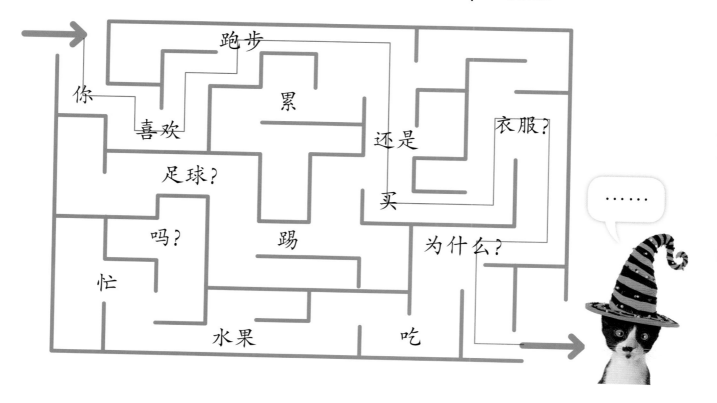

Chant

Listen and say.

朗读儿歌的同时请部分学生配合儿歌内容进行角色扮演。儿歌中出现的衣物老师可以提前准备，使情境更真实，或可在课堂上让学生画出衣物，作为道具。

买衣服、买衣服，

爸爸买长裤，妈妈买上衣，

姐姐买短裤，弟弟买球衣。

买衣服、买衣服，

红裤子好看还是蓝裤子好看？

白球衣好看还是黄球衣好看？

买衣服、买衣服，

红色、蓝色、白色、黄色，

长裤、短裤、上衣、球衣都好看。

生活用语 Daily expressions

忙吗？
Are you busy?

参考对话：
浩浩：爸爸，忙吗？去打球吗？
爸爸：对不起，浩浩。我现在很忙。

听你的！
Up to you!

爱莎：我们喝果汁，还是喝水？
玲玲：听你的！

写一写 Write

1 Trace and write the characters.

、 亠 ナ 亣 衣 衣

丿 刀 月 月 肝 肝 服 服

衣 服	衣 服
衣 服	衣 服

2 Write and say.

这是我的新 衣服 。

我的 衣服 太 大 了。

3 Fill in the blanks with the correct words. Colour the correct presents using the same colours.

绿色

粉色

黄色

今天

令天

为什么

为怎么

他

她

衣服

长服

蓝色

25 DECEMBER
00:01

他 是谁？

他 的红色的 衣服 好看吗？

他 为什么 这么累？

昨天是十二月二十四日，他很忙。

今天 是十二月二十五日，他说："真累！"

拼音输入法 Pinyin input

1　Look at the keyboard. Type the 23 consonants listed on the right.

打字前带领学生将声母朗读一遍，提醒他们不要将声母和英文字母的发音混淆了。

We use the 26 letters on the keyboard to input Pinyin. In the Pinyin system, there are 23 consonants:

b p m f　　zh ch sh r

d t n l　　z c s

g k h　　y w

j q x

2　Now, type the consonants without looking at the list.

多元学习 Connections

Cultures

土耳其的 Grand Bazaar 是全世界最大的有顶集市之一，出售珠宝、地毯、香料、陶瓷、刺绣等物品。在泰国的 Damnoen Saduak 水上市场，小贩们划着小船售卖各种蔬菜水果和其他商品。比利时位于 Place du Jeu de Balle 的跳蚤市场每天都开放，销售各式各样的物品。英国的 Oxford Street 是欧洲最繁华的购物街之一。

Look at the advertisements for some famous shopping spots around the world. Talk about them with your friend.

the Grand Bazaar in Istanbul, Turkey

the Damnoen Saduak floating market in Ratchaburi, Thailand

the flea market at the Place du Jeu de Balle in Brussels, Belgium

Oxford Street in London, UK

参考表达：
我喜欢 the Damnoen Saduak floating market。
因为我爱吃水果。

我喜欢……

因为……

为什么？

完成第一题后，可问问学生是否曾经跟家人通过手机应用程序在网上购物，
并邀请一些学生谈谈他们用过的网上购物应用程序，以此引入第二题。

1 How many of your friends like buying things in shops? How many prefer shopping online? Do a survey and write the numbers.

我喜欢和爸爸妈妈一起去买衣服。

我们喜欢在网上买玩具。

2 Design the home page for a mobile phone shopping application and talk about it with your friend.

My Design

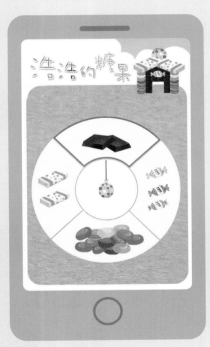

浩浩的糖果

玲玲的天地

玩具		
文具		
书		
衣服		
花		

我喜欢在这里买文具。

这里的糖果很好吃。

你喜欢它吗？为什么？

我……，因为……

参考表达：
我喜欢，因为这里的衣服很多，很好看。

游戏方法：
学生按代金券的面额大小，从最小的 20 元开始完成任务，每正确完成
项任务可获得对应代金券。完成后看看自己一共获得了多少元代金券。

1 Complete the tasks. How many vouchers can you get?

$20

买　　　卖

Read aloud.

$30

$30

星期六，我和
弟弟去跑步。

$30

这是
Answ
这是裤

$50

9 a.m.

3 p.m.

CINEMA

$50

Ask your friend 'Do you like
dogs? Why?' in Chinese.

你喜欢狗吗？
为什么？

$80

$50

你爱做什么？
Look at the pictures
and answer in
Chinese.

我爱跑步和打羽毛球。

$100

Make your parents a cup
of tea and say 'Are
you tired? Please
drink some tea.'
in Chinese.

妈妈比爸爸忙。

我上午打……，……

我上午打篮球，下午看电影。

Write the characters.

衣 服

你们累吗？请喝茶。

评核方法：
学生两人一组，互相考察评价表内单词和句子的听说读写。交际沟通部分由老师朗读要求，学生再互相对话。如果达到了某项技能要求，则用色笔将星星或小辣椒涂色。

2 Work with your friend. Colour the stars and the chillies.

Words and sentences	说	读	写
衣服	☆	☆	☆
裤子	☆	☆	🌶
跑步	☆	☆	🌶
买	☆	☆	🌶
忙	☆	☆	🌶
累	☆	☆	🌶
爱	☆	🌶	🌶
卖	☆	🌶	🌶
运动服	☆	🌶	🌶
电影	☆	🌶	🌶
为什么？	☆	☆	🌶

Talk about shopping experiences	☆
Talk about clothes	☆

3 What does your teacher say?

评核建议：
根据学生课堂表现，分别给予"太棒了！(Excellent!)"、"不错！(Good!)"或"继续努力！(Work harder!)"的评价，再让学生圈出上方对应的表情，以记录自己的学习情况。

分享 Sharing

延伸活动：
1 学生用手遮盖英文，读中文单词，并思考单词意思；
2 学生用手遮盖中文单词，看着英文说出对应的中文单词；
3 学生四人一组，尽量运用中文单词分角色复述故事。

Words I remember

衣服	yī fu	clothes
裤子	kù zi	trousers
跑步	pǎo bù	to run
买	mǎi	to buy
忙	máng	busy
累	lèi	tired
为什么	wèi shén me	why
爱	ài	to like
卖	mài	to sell
运动服	yùn dòng fú	sportswear
电影	diàn yǐng	film

Other words

夏天	xià tiān	summer
了	le	(used to indicate the completion of an action)
条	tiáo	(measure word for something long, narrow or thin)
件	jiàn	piece
路	lù	journey, distance
一下	yī xià	for a while
吧	ba	(used at the end of a sentence to soften the tone)

OXFORD
UNIVERSITY PRESS

Oxford University Press is a department of the University of Oxford.
It furthers the University's objective of excellence in research, scholarship,
and education by publishing worldwide. Oxford is a registered trade mark of
Oxford University Press in the UK and in certain other countries

Published in Hong Kong by
Oxford University Press (China) Limited
39th Floor, One Kowloon, 1 Wang Yuen Street, Kowloon Bay,
Hong Kong

Illustrated by Anne Lee, KK Ng, KY Chan and Wildman

Photographs for reproduction permitted by Dreamstime.com

China National Publications Import & Export (Group) Corporation is an authorized distributor of
Oxford Elementary Chinese.

Please contact content@cnpiec.com.cn or 86-10-65856782

ISBN: 978-0-19-942997-4

10 9 8 7 6 5 4 3 2

Teacher's Edition
ISBN: 978-0-19-082262-0

10 9 8 7 6 5 4 3 2